THE CRIES OF FREEDOM PAST & PRESENT

POEMS THAT TELL STORIES OF MIXED EMOTIONS OF FREEDOM and LIFE ISSUES

BY PAULINE J. SCHLOSS

authorHOUSE®

AuthorHouse™
1663 Liberty Drive
Bloomington, IN 47403
www.authorhouse.com
Phone: 1-800-839-8640

First published by AuthorHouse 5/11/2009

ISBN: 978-1-4389-7003-5 (sc)

Printed in the United States of America
Bloomington, Indiana

This book is printed on acid-free paper.

THE CRIES OF FREEDOM

PAST & PRESENT

The poems that deals with the past, tell stories of different thoughts from different people, on what freedom meant to them when slavery was abolished.

Poems of the present address life issues and struggles that continue to be a part of our everyday life.

PAULINE J. SCHLOSS

ACKNOWLEDGMENT

I wish to thank God for the inspiration He has given to me to create words with the purpose of changing minds, to convict and correct, not only in my life but also in others. I hope that this book will help to acknowledge the different emotions of our forefathers as they struggle to understand the word 'freedom'

I thank my children Leron, Edmarie, Marsha, Kadian, Myrtle, and Alrick, for their encouragement in the writing of this book. I also wish to acknowledge my step-children, my sons in- law and my daughters in-laws. Special mention to Olivia, Jasmine, Chelsea, Samuel and Joseph, my grandchildren, I love you all very much.

To Marlene Ffrench, Marcia Grey, Jean Powell, Edward L. Brown and Donald Downer who were always there as constant sources of support and encouragement.

Last, but not the least among the pack, I wish to thank my editors, Patricia Ffrench and Edmarie Edwards with their keen insights. They were able to give life to the words. I wish also to thank Norman Hemming for the final touch that gave wings to the written words.

WITH ALL HIS BLESSING THANKS A MILLION!

DEDICATION

I would like to dedicate this book to my grand children,
to my great grand children, and their children,
that they will always enjoy 'freedom'
and never take it for granted.

"TO CRY FREEDOM

IS

TO

KNOW FREEDOM,

SO

HOW

CAN

I

CRY?"

CONTENTS

slave quarters on plantation

My Story, Your Grandfather's Story, and Your Son's Story.

I was twelve years old when I was captured and was sold to the strange men with the pale skin wearing strange clothes. My life as I knew it was changed forever. I lost my family, my name, my roots, I almost lost myself, that is how lost I was.

As I was hauled away, I remembered my mother, beautiful and proud. She was the daughter of the Chief, my grandfather. My father was as brave as the mighty Zulu of the olden days. I was confident that he would find me. Remembering my roots, I could not lose myself; I became a warrior that day with a will to fight, not knowing whom to fight.

It all happened when I went to the woods to get some sticks for the fire. Listening to the beautiful sounds of the birds, as the early morning sunbeams flashed across my face. I smiled not knowing that the next minute would be the beginning of the darkest journey of my life. The shedding of my dreams and the fading memories of my family and culture all started that day. Years later, I realized that, that day I was condemned to be a 'boy' forever. I would never know what it was to be called a man, or to be recognized as one.

I got up that morning with the desire to please my mother; I wanted to get her some fire sticks for her to cook for the big feast planned for that night. As children we were told of the danger of going to the woods alone. Suddenly I felt afraid, looking around I realized that I wandered too far from home without my friends. Suddenly I heard the breaking of sticks, I stopped, and I listened. The birds suddenly took flight; I knew that, that was a sure sign that someone was near. I felt alarmed, I turned to find a hiding place, but I was too late. Someone held onto

3

me from behind. Their footsteps I did not hear, the hands that held me were the same color as mine. However, the tongue spoken was different, I did not understand.

My warrior instinct was to fight, I tried, but I was overpowered. Bounded and gagged I was taken far away from my village.

Along the way, others like me were added to the long walk to the unknown. I saw fear in their eyes. I knew that my eyes reflected theirs. I thought about my mother, "what was she thinking, what would she do without her beloved son?' I am her first child. My father will start a war with our neighbors; he would think they were the ones who have captured me. I wondered to myself, what I can do. Where were they taking me?'

We walked for many moons, adding daily more people, some from my own village. We were not allowed to walk together or talk to each other.

We had to carry water, bundles of corn, elephant tusks and baskets with things we could not see.

We were handed over to people I did not know, men who looked like the gods. They had long knives and long sticks that gave off smoke and a loud sound; I saw it kill a boy who tried to get away. Can you imagine a little black boy looking at these strange pale skin men with long hair? They were wearing funny clothes and hats. These people did not resemble me or anyone I have ever seen. They must have dropped from the sky. I was so afraid, I was shaking with terror. My mother and father must be looking for me; I was so far away from home. I looked around to see a way to escape, but there was none.

The tribesmen were trading copper pots, beads, knives for each slave. Two copper pots, two knives were exchanged for me; someone told them that I was the grandson of a chief. After the exchange we were placed in canoes to be taken to the big boat. When I saw the big boat, my heart became so small; it was as if it was not there anymore. At that moment I lost hope of ever seeing my kinfolk again. I begged shamelessly for them to let me go, I told them that my grandfather would give them gold. I only knew my own language so I used it. They did not understand me. The more I cried and kicked, the more they laughed. They were shocked to see tears coming from me. The pale men did not know that I could cry.

On the Ship

We were placed in the bottom of the big boat, we were so packed.

We could not move nor look behind. All body functions took place there. The smell was awful. Cries of anger, and of pain, echoed everywhere. People from everywhere were chained together, all with the same look of sorrow.

I lost count of the many moons as we went farther away from the land of my birth. There were always thoughts of death on our minds. I tried not eating and I was flogged so badly I could hardly move. Some of the fighting men were chained together with a large fish net over them. This was done to prevent them from throwing themselves overboard.

On this particular day, we were given permission to come up on deck for some fresh air. Suddenly the heavens opened and the rain started. The boat started to rock, water deluged the deck as rain cascaded in seemingly endless torrents. Shouts of fear and anger were coming from the savages. They started to throw stuff overboard, human beings were no exception. They threw anyone and anything they got their hands on. I stayed out of their way, paling water from the deck. I learned to listen, and to understand their strange tongue.

I suddenly heard cries of despair and shouts of freedom as a beautiful woman, like my mother, jumped overboard. She chose death rather than the bed of all these savages. I cried in my heart as lives changed forever right in front of my eyes. I can no longer see the land of my forefathers. But, I still hear the cries of my mother and the anguish moans of my father. I can still hear the battle cries of my grandfather, willing to fight. But whom does he fight. I see my grandmother praying to the unknown god for my safe return.

The sea rages as if it was angry with the gods. The strange men throw humans overboard, as if they were feeding the fury of the sea.

For a moment I imagine my mother telling her story, my story.

I heard cries and hurried footsteps; the boys came to my door, the ones that were sent with Prince Salu. They were so frightened; they fell to the ground speechless. My heart took a leap and started to beat so hard I heard it above the cries of the boys.

"My son! my son! , where is my son?" I shouted to the boys.

No answer came, only the wailing of the women who by now gather around the boys. From a distance I heard the cries of war from the men, my husband among them.

I slowly lower myself to the floor, asking once again in a whispering tone.

"Where is my son? Where is Prince Salu?

Then I heard myself scream;

"Find him! Don't just stand there!"

"Find my beloved son!"

One brave boy spoke, "he was captured by pale men, men with long sticks that kill when smoke comes out with a big bang.

"Oh, Queen Mother, Prince Salu fought like a warrior, he really tried to get away, spoke another".

I held my hands up to the heavens and screamed the name of my beloved son.

I wanted the pale men to hear the cry of a broken mother whose child was taken.

I cried for my son and hoped the wind would carry my voice.

I know within my heart that my son heard and captured the sound of my voice; my voice that will give him the will to fight as a warrior and to return to me one day.

I imagine my father.

I imagine my father wanting to fight, but whom?
I imagine my father who has killed ten lions.
Fighting the animals and, foes of the village,
to ensure our safety.
Today, this hour, he stood with the warriors of our village ready to fight.
But whom does he fight?
He beats his chest
He jumped high in rage.
He cannot cry.

A warrior does not cry.
My father beats his chest in an effort to remove the pain from his heart,
To released the anguish of his being.
He jumped high to seek the faces of the gods,
while he cried out to them for me.
But in his heart, he cries to the unknown God of the universe.
He shouted to the boys who were with me.
He wanted to blame someone, anyone.
He wanted to know why me?
He protected me from the wilds of the land.
He could not protect me from the pale strange men of the sea.

Amidst the cries of my fellow men,
I heard my fathers' cry carried by the wind, I took strength from it.
I held unto it.
I knew then, I will survive.
I shall return to the land of my birth, my roots, my language, my culture.
I shall return.
When and how I ponder not.

On The Ship

ON BOARD A SLAVE-SHIP.

I came to the Land of the Unknown

I came to the land of the unknown,
with the known, fading as swiftly
as the big boat that took us across
the mighty angry waters.

I came to the land of unknown,
with no hope, no dreams.
It was hard to hold onto dreams,
when the reality of the present
was foreign to me.
I had no hope.

I came to the land of the unknown,
with no pride, no thoughts of being a brave warrior.
I came with only the thought that
I must maintain freedom in my heart.
I came, holding on to my culture, my roots,
trying hard to remember who I am.

I came to this land, with the will to survive,
because, I am my 'Father's son'.
The son of the bravest' man,
'My grandfather'
Their blood ran through my vein.
The blood of the free.
I know I am a free man in chains.
That thought, gave me the will to survive
in the land of the unknown.

P.J>SCHLOSS

To love is to experience freedom.

To hate, is to experience bondage.

P.J. Schloss.

You Never Had Me.

'You bought me.
You did not own me.

You lie with me
You did not have me.

You whipped me
You did not break me.

You try to quench my emotions
You did not succeed.

I had your child.
He was not yours.

I had my dreams.
They are were not yours.

When I cry,
They are were my tears, not yours.

When I dance and sing,
It's the culture of my forefathers.
Not yours.

When I speak in the depths of my heart
of my hope for freedom
It's not your words that form my thoughts,
There are mine.
The language of my people.

In fact I was always free,
Because I choose, not to allow you,
to enslave my spirit or my heart.

P.J.SCHLOSS

'LET US CRY UNTIL FREEDOM IS
AWAKEN IN OUR BEING,

IT IS ONLY THEN THAT WE CAN TRULY
HOPE, DREAM AND LOVE".

P.J. SCHLOSS

My Bag

My bag is packed
My mule is ready.
Mek me go before
Massa change 'im mind.
Me no find no honor in a 'im word
My bag is packed
My mule is ready
The road before me
I am ready to go
But where?

P.J>SCHLOSS

Tell Me Father

Tell me Father,
how can we be free,
when we still look at Massa's feet?
Waiting with bended shoulders,
For the crack of the whip?

How can we be free?
when the scars are healed on the outside?
But on the inside, there are open
and raw with desire for revenge.

How can we be free?
when we cannot read and write?
or, even able to count the money of the free.?
So please tell me,
for whom did freedom come.?
For us? or, for the white man with a conscience?

I know Father, that you don't know the answers.
Yet, I have to ask.
Maybe, one day our kinfolk will have the answers.

Father, I have one more question,
Tell me;
"How can we be free when our spirits are still enslaved?

P.J>SCHLOSS

What Is Freedom?

How can I cry freedom?
When I can't recognize the word.
When I can't comprehend the word,
When I don't know what freedom really is.

Tell me, what is freedom?
Is it only to be free from whipping?
Is it to be free from the selling of our children?
Is it freedom from the fields?
Tell me what is freedom?

Answer me this question;
Is there freedom outside this plantation?
When one cannot read the signs at the crossroads,
Or, am I just free to stand in the middle
wondering which way to go?

How can I cry freedom?
When there is no liberty in my heart?
Only fear of the unknown.
Only doubt in the testing of my strength.
My whole being cries to be free.

But I am too afraid to set it free.
Just because I don't know what freedom really is?
I am only **an'x'** to the world, so how can I cry freedom.

P.J>SCHLOSS

I Leap

As the bells of freedom rings
I leap high in the sky
willing myself to fly.

To reach for the stars
To give me light in the dark
For a new start.

I seek the clouds to be my roof,
as I walked among the roots.
The rain, I ask to give me water when I thirst,
As I take a taste of freedom first.

With joy I leap
Knowing God has provided me a heap.
He knows that one day I would need,
all that He has in His keep.

P.J>SCHLOSS

I Am Free

Today I am free
Free to dance,
Free to sing
To cry
To love
To sleep
To eat
Free to hug my child
Free to love my man
to choose whom to lie with.

Yes, today I am free to dream of my motherland.
To speak my native tongue.
To remember the taste of my native food.
Yes, three hundred years have passed
In my mind it's like three years.
Yes, I am free.
Yes, I know that freedom has a price
Yet, I am willing to pay
to ensure the continued ring of freedom.

Freedom is precious; it's a gift of life.
Paid in full by the blood of our forefathers.
Their spirits spoke to mine, telling me to dance,
To sing songs of praises to the Father above.

The spirits of old held hands,
They dance all day and night
Because, today their spirits are free.

P.J>SCHLOSS

Come Everyone

Come everyone
Let's sing and dance.
This is the day to rejoice.
This day that we have long waited for, has come.
For this day our forefathers have died.

Grab your daughter
Your son
Your man
Your woman
Everyone, friends, mothers, fathers.

Let's dance in unity.
Let's share our love one to another.
Let's share our strength with our weaker ones.
Come everyone.
Let's sing and dance.
Let's dance the night away.

P.J>SCHLOSS

Maasai Mara men

To know and accept Jesus is to know and experience true freedom.—

If you are free by Jesus, you are free indeed.

John 8:32

Freedom has always been in my Heart.

Freedom is in my heart
Free as the flow of tears that washes
away the power of hate.
That breaks the vengeance,
I hold against those that hold my body in captivity.

Freedom has always been in my heart;
When I hold my head high;
My shoulders straight,
trying hard to master unflinching courage
as the crack of the whip hiss the air,
landing on my board ebony back.

Freedom is in my heart, when I answer, 'yes massa,'
when I ran to do his bidding.
It is in my heart where it cannot be reached to be
enslaved.
I know that I am free,
because my father told me that to be truly free
is to embrace love that will allow freedom to grow in
the heart.
And I did.

My heart has a song' a song of freedom.
A song I can freely sing today.
The freedom I had embrace in my heart
is now free to take wings and fly.

P.J.>SCHLOSS

They Took Us

They took us from our land.
Sold us
Used us.
Beat us
Took everything that is humanly possible.
Our name
Our history
Our roots.
Our women
Our manhood.
Now 250 years later, the word is out,
'Freedom is here'

Now what?
No payment for our loss and suffering?
No payment for years of working for free.
No thought of the shedding of our family?
No apologies?

Freedom will not be easy.
The white man has lost his domain.
He will now excise his authority
in a different and cruel way.
Freedom for us is bondage under the law.
The white's man law.

I see no freedom in sight.
Not the reality of it.
I need to know my history
I need to recapture my dignity.
I need to know the meaning of being a man
And not a boy, then and only then I will know freedom.

PJ.> SCHLOSS.

A Runaway

I am a runaway.
The quest for freedom has always been in my heart.
I have been whipped,
I have been bound in chains and shackles, yet I ran,
mostly in my heart.

Today, I heard the cry of freedom.
There is no need to run, freedom has found me.
I can now walk and not run.
I am no longer a runaway.
I am now a free man.
No tag, no whip, no chain, no shackles.

Yet, the quest for freedom still lingers in my heart.
I question, why do you linger?
Freedom is here.
Can I not be set free?
I have no need to run.

Then, I was questioned,
"Are you free from the haunting thoughts of your
yesterdays?
Thoughts of revenge?
Thoughts of hate against those,
that held you and your forefathers in captivity?.
Those that rape your women.? Sold your children?"

"Are you free to embrace love, joy, peace, and
forgiveness?
Are you running now, from the captive thoughts that
aim to bring
you into another type of captivity?"

They have set your physical being free.
You alone can free your mind from being a runaway.
Set yourself free and embrace the freedom that is
given.
Conquer the quest with peace.

PJ>SCHLOSS

The Old

The old found new strength
new vigor and rhythm to dance.
To sing songs of victory from the 'Motherland'.

Songs that were passed down through the ages,
in the dead of night.
The old found the songs
that were stored deep in the heart.

So today, they remember without fear,
Without the sounds that drowns out memories.
The cries of pain,
from the cracking of the whip.
The cry of the mother
as her child is taken from her breast.
The groan of anguish,
as a father is taken from his family.
The wailing of a young girl,
as she lost her virginity to uninvited lust.

The old held onto the reality that today,
they are free to mourn.
Free to bury their dead, their way.
Free to cry for their pain.
For their lost child, husband, mother, father,
Free to call their names, to feel their loneliness.

The old heard the cry of freedom.
Their hearts leap with renewed hope.
Faded dreams for their young ones
became bright once more.
Hope became the sunrise in their lives.

Yet the old, does not know how to pass on their dreams
to the youth of the free.
Freedom has given them wings to fly.

P.J.>SCHLOSS

25

My Free Paper.

I was given my free paper
by my massa, father.
He said, "You are free to go."

But where?
I am mixed
Black and white
I do not belong any where.
No roots.

I reminded my mother
of the night she was raped.
I reminded my father,
he disgraced his redneck race.

With paper in hand,
I wonder where I belong.
Where do I go?

P.J>SCHLOSS

The Chain

The chain fell today, giving freedom.
Not only from my waist,
But also from my heart.

I choose to embrace liberty in my heart.
Gaining strength to face a new tomorrow.

I know;
My mother told me
Only the truly free can embrace the sunrise,
and the sunset of their lives.

P.J>SCHLOSS

Hand Of God.

I spend sleepless nights
praying to God for this day.
Now it is here,
I wonder what to do?

I will rise and take hold
of the hand of God.
We will go together
into this land of the free.

With God by my side,
I am free indeed.

P.J>SCHLOSS

Freedom Day

I am singing the song of freedom.
My voice rings from field to field.
Carried by the wind to the big house
From the south to the north
From the east to the west.
This song of freedom must be heard.

Yes, I am free.
Not only by my spoken words.
But also by my fallen tears.
Now, I am free to sing
I am free to dance.
I am free to be the woman
I always wanted to be.

My sisters, join hands with me.
Put down your woes my brothers,
Lift your voice and sing.
Give voice to the song of freedom in your heart.
Sing in this land of the free.
Enjoy the air of freedom.

I dance in circle with arms open wide,
Head lifted up, daring the wind of the free
To give me wings to fly with glee.

As I dance to the fast rhythm of the Congo drums,
My thoughts went even faster.
I was not willing to listen to the voices of tomorrow's
reality.
Questions came, that I need not ponder on today's
actuality.
The only word I allow to surface is 'freedom'

P.J>SCHLOSS

slaves cultivating sugar canes in the West Indies

FREEDOM IS LOVE.

FREEDOM IS FORGIVING EVEN WHEN
IT HURTS.

FREEDOM IS FINDING YOUR PURPOSE
AND ACTING ON IT.

P.J.SCHLOSS.

Air Of Freedom.

Yes, today I am free.
Let me enjoy the air of freedom.
I will inhale and exhale this fresh gush of freedom wind.

Hush; allow me to listen to the shouts of joy.
I will embrace the joy of the moment.

Hear the melody of the birds,
who give music to the song of freedom
For tomorrow it could be the cry of anguish.

Look, see the trees gently moving from side to side
Giving honor to this day of freedom
They are free too.
They no longer have to bear the burden
of the heart that breaks at their roots.

Nor, do they have to hear the cracking of the whip.
As men try hard to bear their lifeless bodies on their
branches.
Yes, the trees are free.
I am free.
Yes, today I am free.

P.J>SCHLOSS

Lord You Have Blessed Me.

Lord, You have blessed my ears.
Today, I am hearing the beautiful cry of freedom.

Lord, You have blessed my eyes to see,
this wonderful day of joy.

Lord, You have blessed my feet
I can dance the dance of my motherland.

Lord, You have blessed my mouth,
I can speak of your faithfulness.

Lord, You have blessed my voice
I can sing praises to your name and to your mighty
acts.

Lord, You have blessed me with the knowledge
that my children and their generation to come are free.

Lord, You have blessed me,
when I cry it will not be of sorrow, but happiness.
The word 'choice' has awake in my being.

Lord, You have blessed me today,
When I die I will carry the message of victory to tell the
folks of old.
They went with sadness, regrets, sorrows, lost dreams
and faded hopes.

Lord, you have blessed me today.
I joined hands with my brothers and sisters to build a
fence of love and unity.
To nurture hope within the fold, on this day of freedom.
Lord, You have blessed me today.

P.J>SCHLOSS

The Cry

The cry echoes from the valley to the mountain top,
over the hills and into the towns.
And from the towns, to the big cities.

This beautiful sound was carried by the wind,
enhanced by the beats of the drums.
Reaching down to each valley
to enfold each joyous cry.
To add to the message of hope,
coming from the beats of the drums.

The rhythms of the drums are joyful.
But they were not of a wedding.
They carried messages of hope, victory,
new dreams and of sadness.
Messages, that every black man
and woman needs to know.

The drums, brought messages of fear
and resentment to some white folks.
To others, it was a feeling of relief.
A freedom of guilt from their hearts.

As the sound of the drums became stronger
strengthened by the joyous cries of the people,
The message became clearer and dearer
to the hearts of the captive.
To some it sounded like a dream.

Some gladly embrace the reality that today
the drums and the wind have brought,
'Messages of hope'.

P.J>SCHLOSS

I Remembered

I remembered the cries of freedom.
I heard the joyous beats of the drums.
The beats, that drowns out the fear
that lingers in my heart.

I saw ladies dancing,
lifting their skirts high above their heads.
Not caring that their wares were seen.

I saw men dropping their hoes;
as the cries of freedom reached their ears.
With hands on their hips;
Heads lifted up with manly pride.
And with everything that gives sound: pots, pans.
They join the joyous cries.

I shook my head, seeking reality.
Do they realize the price that was paid for this
freedom?
Do they really understand the word freedom?
Do they know nothing is really free?
There is always a price to pay.

I laughed; we have already paid the price.
I dance with my kinfolk.
Blocking the cares of tomorrow,
While embracing the joys of the moment.

P.J>Schloss

Look at them

Look at them!
They are dancing, singing, and beating their drums.
For what? Freedom?
Do they know what freedom means?

Do they understand that they will
have to find their own
food, clothes, shelter?.
Where will they find jobs? money?
Do they think I am going to pay for
what I use to get for free?
Do they know what freedom means?

I have lost money!
I have lost control
I have lost prestige
I am no longer a slave owner.

Are they aware that, this freedom
does not come with any rights?
Poor bastards!
What are they thinking?
How will they know the laws?
When they cannot read or write.

Yet, here they are singing and dancing,
without a care for tomorrow .
I guess people needed to be free,
even if death and starvation are the open doors.

P.J>SCHLOSS

My Free Mind

I shook my head,
Trying hard to disregard the negative thoughts
Of the past, present and the future.
Freeing my mind to embrace the positive.

I shook my head,
Struggling to free my mind,
to listen to the plans for the future.
To hold onto the hope that,
there is a better tomorrow,
where dreams can become reality.

P.J>SCHLOSS.

Little Joe

Little Joe hurried from the field with hands spread out from each side, seeking balance, swinging from side to side giving one a sense of urgency.
His scars harden back now bended to the shape of the load he carried every hour, every day, for sixty years. The harden scars are from the whipping he received when he was too weary to go on, too hungry to lift the load on to his shoulders.

Little Joe heard the cry, the joyous cry of freedom and it gave him renewed hope, new dreams, new desires, oh, what a feeling! It was pure joy. He hurried to find his drums that he had built with his own hands to play on a day such as this. Little Joe had a mission, he had to get the news to the kinfolk in the 'Mother Land' that captivity has fallen and freedom has come.

Little Joe beats the drums the old way, in a joyous way. He beats it with all his heart and soul. In giving his all to the beating of the drums he hopes that somehow the message of joy will reach the 'mother land' that was raped of her sons and daughters. He wants everyone to know that freedom has come at last. He thought of the men and women of old that their bodies are now free to receive the spirits that lingers in the motherland.
His fingers could not move fast enough, he wanted every one from continent to continent, island to island to know, and to celebrate with him, that today he has the taste of freedom and it is good.

Love Is Freedom

I will live in my heart where there is love.
Because where there is love, there is freedom.
Where there is liberty, much love abounds.
I will live in my heart where I find love,

I will live in your world, share the air you breathe.
Share the sunshine and the rain.
I will even try to exit in your culture,
where I see and experience more hate than love.

I will hold fast to the love in my heart.
I will shut the door to hate
I will erase thoughts of revenge.
I want to love, I want to be free.
I want to be a man.
Then, and only then, I will be willing to share my love.

P.J>Schloss

The Boy

The boy ran crying out to his grandpapa.
What is freedom?
What? my son.
Listen grandpapa them singing, 'Freedom, Freedom'
What is freedom?

Are we free as the birds that fly in the sky?
That sings in the blue sunny sky?
Or as the dogs that run over the fields?
Are we free to go through the big gate
without Massa and the dogs coming after us?
Tell me grandpa, 'are we free to sit by the river to fish?'

Grandpapa, answer me, "what is freedom?'
"I don't know son,
I never knew the meaning of that word.
But for you son, this is a new word,
go, embrace it, find the meaning.
Allow it to treat you well,
you now have a choice,
a choice I did not have.
You now have a choice to use
this new found freedom in a good or bad way".
"Thanks grandpa, I will remember your words."

P.J>SCHLOSS

I am not your Girl

Today I have become a woman
I am not your girl anymore.
I don't have to count my toes anymore,
while I wait for your name calling to stop.
Today is freedom.
I don't have to cook.
I don't have to clean.
I don't have to sew.
Now your tears can water your rose garden.
I don't have to be hurt by your thorns anymore.
And best of all I don't have to lie with your man
anymore.

Today I rejoice
Today I dance
Today I sing
Today I embrace freedom with all that it has to offer
Good or bad.
Come what may tomorrow, I am no longer your girl.
I am my own woman.
I am free.

P.J>SCHLOSS

"TO FORGET OUR HISTORY;

IS TO FORGET

THE VALUE of

FREEDOM"

Pauline J Schloss.

The Struggle Continues,
To Free
The Enslaved Hearts And Minds.

This is January 1, 1965. It has been 100 years since the cries of freedom echoed through the plantations, over the hills and in the towns. It was 100 years ago that we were promised a mule and forty acres of land when we were freed. It is still unknown to me how many people came into this promise. It has been 100 years and people are still being lynched.

I still do not understand the word 'freedom' and why they said we had it.

I sat in the barber shop and listened to the stories being told and I wondered were we ever free? It has been 100 years since we were told that we are free, but we are still sitting in the back of the bus. Our black men are still boys in the eyes of the whites. The white men still think that our black women are their property for them to do whatever, whenever. No one arrests them for rape, the blacks could not testify against them and their peers would not tell. We see the little half white children, (whom the whites call black) running all over the place. The children are without fathers, without names, without roots, and without justice for their mothers.

The word 'freedom' is not known in the streets, when we cannot walk on the sidewalk if a white person approaches. We are still looking from the outside in. Some restaurants are off limits to us blacks, even if we are famous, and accomplished. We are still called the 'N' word.

White schools are still closed to our children. We are still not free to go into certain towns or neighborhoods, unless you are the maid or the yard man and even then, you are still required to carry a pass.

Even the poorest uneducated white person thinks they are better than the educated blacks.

We still cannot walk, talk, and sleep the way our heart desires. Fear sits where freedom should reign, so where is freedom? .

Each day the question of, 'what is freedom?' surfaces in the black bars, in songs, over the dining table, in the barber shops, everywhere people gather, the question pops up. My people still do not understand the word, because there is no experience of being free and so they cannot apply it to their everyday life.

Every day you hear of the most horrid stories of lynching. Just last week we heard of Grandma Rose's grandson being lynched because he wanted to vote. Although we have no rights and no talk, we still have our culture, the culture of our forefathers. We had to hold on to our culture and we stored it in our hearts where no one could take it. If the white man could have taken it, he would have, and our spirits would have been broken. We would be wiped from the face of this country. Our culture and religion gave us hope, the will to survive and to stand for what we believe in.

Words came from the north that the new President is planning to make changes, changes that will be of benefit to the 'black man.'

Words also came from the south that the black Baptist Minster, Rev. King continues to speak out, but there is fear for his life. He was put in prison more than once, his house was set on fire, but he did not stop fighting for what he believed in. He did not show his fear to his enemies; he looked to God to keep him until his purpose was fulfilled.

We as a people still wait to breathe the air of freedom; to sleep with the thought of freedom, to eat with the taste of freedom, to love with freedom in our hearts, this will enable us to live in unity. I still hear the cries of freedom of my forefathers, wanting us in this generation to fulfill the reality of freedom, as men, not as boys, as women, not as girls.

We need to feel that we are really sitting in the front of the bus.

We need to be united as one to hold on to freedom.

To find and know your purpose is
good;

To fulfill your purpose, is to live your
life to the fullest.

PJ.>Schloss

Dr. Martin Luther King Jr.

His voice was low and even
yet, impressive.
Lingering, waiting to be sure everyone understands.
Only confidence speaks in his voice.
His movements were not pushy.
Authority walks in each step.
With a purpose one cannot soon forget.

His heart warms to everyone within his reach.
His words, he hopes everyone understands.
To enfolded within their hearts,
that there is hope for tomorrow.

His eyes mirror his soul full of God's love.
For each within, and out of his fold.
His winning smile breaks down barriers.
Opening doors to heads of state, kings and Queens.
With all his fame he knew whom he served,
and his purpose here on earth.

P.J>SCHLOSS.

Blue Mountain Cries

High gleaming mountain standing proud
with sunshine of gold.
Leaping to touch the young and the old.
Enfolding the laughter,
while enjoying the songs of the daughters.

This land I protect.
This land I will not reject.
This land of healing screams
This land with herb's for the ailing souls.
Yet, I stood high, basking in sunshine of gold.
Thinking of the past, men of old.

My brothers stood, not as high, as dark clouds hover.
Sadness mingles with dark thoughts.
Not hearing the laughter of the daughters
but the cries of the mothers.
Wailing as the blood of the brothers ran
to meet those of the fathers.
My brother mountain cries,
"Stop the killing,
Let joy and peace begin
Have you forgotten God?"
Have guns and knives become your god.
Look around, color has gone from the land.
Songs have died on the lips.
Laughter no longer lingers in the air.
Only smoke from the guns.

Man has grown cold.
Just as the song and laughter of the soul.
My other brother mountain holds hope for
the healing of the land.
Hoping sons and daughters
will reach out with the gift of hope
To restore lost dreams,
to renew their spirit with love.

I stand proud to be known
as the Blue Mountain of this land.
This land I will protect
This land I will not reject
This land of wood and water.
Jamaica, land we love.

P.J.>SCHLOSS

Bondage in the land

There is no freedom in the land.
The daughter's tears are mingled with fears.
The sons' sweats have been replaced with blood.

Old men sit with folded hands, with lost hope.
With no will to rise, to reclaim the land.

Old women cry with broken hearts
for God to remove
the evil bondage that has taken hold of their children.
There is no freedom in the land.

The land has become hard,
hard as the hearts of men.
Dry as the emotions of a shamed woman.
"How can I cry freedom?
When, even the ear distrusts the word."

When cries echo, mocking the sound,
asking for the souls of sons and daughters of the land.
Souls that were lost in the evil of the land.

How can I cry freedom?
When even the water runs deep fearing to surfaces,
Not wanting to face the dry parched land.
or to mix with the blood of the land.
The land of bondage, full of evil,
needs to be free.

P.J>SCHLOSS

Rift Valley, Kenya

My Strong Man.

My strong beautiful man does not understand freedom.
He does not know how to love freely.

He is afraid to love and to receive love.
He is afraid of commitment.

He is afraid to be the man of his house.
He does not know how to become the lord of his wife.

My strong handsome man cannot enjoy freedom.
He was never free.

P.J>SCHLOSS.

Black Moses

He is our black Moses.
He is our leader of the oppressed
He was sent to deliver, to correct, and to convict.
He was sent with a message of hope.
To point this generation,
to the pathway of freedom.
Of unity and strength in a peaceful way.

He was not afraid to dream
He was not afraid to speak of his dreams.
He taught us to do the same.
Our black Moses empowered us with love
to break down discrimination.

His voice was strong.
It was powerful.
It reaches people of all nations
He is the voice of our people.
He is our black Moses,
He came to set us free,
He is Dr. Martin Luther King Jr.

P.J>SCHLOSS

How can I Cry?

How can I cry for my beloved land?
When there is no one to hear.
The daughters are too numb with fear for living.
The sons are fighting hard to become men in cities
foreign to them.
They missed the cry carried by the wind.
The wind has no place to anchor.

How can I cry?
When mothers are busy weeping for their daughters,
Who are not yet women, but have become mothers.
Fathers hang their heads in shame for the sons who
have forgotten the land.
The land in which their forefathers have toiled since
time began.
Seeking only to become man,
by the hand, and not by the land.

How can I cry?
For this my beloved land.
When man has forgotten the land,
And the land has become hardened to man.
Man has become the land, hard and bitter refusing to
forgive, to love, to trust.
Land has become man, hard and brittle, refusing to
yield the fruit of the land.

Yet I cry, not for the past, but for the present where
hopes lie.
For the future, where dreams will become reality.
Yes, I will cry for this my beloved land.

P.J>SCHLOSS.

Without Roots

Look! A host of people walking
No strength to run.
Cries were heard,
but the words were not.
Are there words to describe the killing of our children?
Tell us a word that can describe the agony of being
enslaved.
Or being uprooted from your land?.

Some cries were hushed, covered
by the pain of the physical, and that of the heart.
The pain was too much, there were no words.

Some cries were subdued,
Moaning and groaning took over.
The weak were too weak to comprehend.
Words were lost.

The strong were too burdened to speak,
Seeking a land of their own
helping the weak, embracing the young.
While keeping their strength, to hold the enemies at bay.

The crows hover, waiting on the weak to fall.
The flies' buzzing, mocks the helpless
and shouts that they are free,
the humans are not.

A host of people with no roots.
Running without hope. With cries, but no words,
With pain and no healing,
With hunger and no food.
With thirst and no water.
With enemies of same color waiting to kill.

A host of people seeking freedom with little hope.
Only with a will to survive, with the grace of Jesus.

P.J>SCHLOSS

57

Maasai Mara ladies

'TO EMBRACE FREEDOM IS TO KNOW
FREEDOM :

NOT ONLY BY THE SPOKEN WORD,

BUT ALSO WITHIN THE HEART'.

P.J>SCHLOSS

I Knew

I knew that when the spirit is free;
The physical being is also free.
The mind is free.

Dreams are given birth.
Hope is renewed.
And the quest for a brighter tomorrow becomes alive,
Like the gust of a refreshing wind in the sunshine.
New hope
New dreams
With love around.

P.J>SCHLOSS

Cry For Your Beloved Land

Cry for your beloved land
the land of your birth.
The land that was brought,
with the blood of your forefathers.

Cry away the shame
Cry away the fear
Cry away the grief
Cry away the distrust
.
I want to say, 'Hush, don't cry'
But why?
Why not cry, until new life is given birth
in this our beloved land.
The land of your birth.

P.J>SCHLOSS.

We Stand and Let.

There is no smile on the parch lips.
The face does not remember how to smile.
The muscles are as hard, as the sun bake land.
There is no song in the aching heart.

The word 'run' does not relate to the legs.
Food is foreign to the stomach as water to the lips.
Birds migrate from the land seeking sound of laughter.
The crows remain silent as the vultures they are, seeking
the sound of slaughter.
How can they survive without music for the soul?
without food? without water?

They?
Yes them! The ones we stand and watch as their souls
are taken.
As their bodies return to dust'
Generation of blood flow, mingle with tears as their
roots, hopes, dreams are lost.
Reality is clear; they are being chase from their land by
their own.

We in the free, stand a mile away, looking through the
glass tube.
Not willing to face reality, too afraid to touch.

Yet we clap and give thanks that
one in a hundred is willing to stand for the cause.
Let it be them not us.
They are not our concerns;
we only want their stuffs oil, gold, copper, diamonds,
animals.
They have our wants.
We have their needs 'Food'

P.J.>SCHLOSS

Our Symbol of Freedom!

It has been 143 years since the cries of freedom were heard.

It was hard to get rid of 4 million people without roots, without a language of their own, or even full knowledge of another land. We are still here, finding our way, making our marks.

Remember, it all started in 1619 when the first 23 slaves landed in James Town. By 1865, 254 years later, over 4 million displace people, without roots, most without education or skill, without language of origin, little knowledge of their culture, no sense of family unit, with no work discipline without the whip, was granted freedom. With little in hand, we started on a journey to find our self, to establish our self, to know our self and our potential. We used our skills in music and sportsmanship to break down barriers. We have been to space; we have invented many things that are of benefit to all people. We have doctors, actors, teachers, own talk shows, business owners, to name a few.
We have a finger in every pie. We have come a long way.

In this year of our Lord, my eyes have seen, my ears have heard and I stood in line for five hours to vote for a black man for president of this the United States of America. I stood for seven hours to bear witness to history, not all for me but for those who had passed and for those to come. I saw black and white holding hands, tears running shamelessly down faces, tears of joy, tears of change, tears of hope, tears of unity. We became one, on that day January 20, 2009 at 12 o' clock as we stood and watch Mr. Barack Obama sworn in as the First black President of the United States.

We have now seen freedom, tasted freedom and know the meaning of freedom. We will walk the road of freedom with this man.

"May God be with him always".

The Promise Land.

The light is getting brighter each day.
Forcing its' way, shattering the darkness.
The sun is rising in all its' glory announcing a new dawn.
The moon is full and at its' brightest.
No need for the lamp; we have seen the light!

There is music in the air. Not only from the birds,
but from men who have seen the light.
From the yearning souls of the spirit man,
those who die with longing in their beings.
The songs in their hearts have finely being set free.

Our Joshua has taken his place.
Our promise land is being shape into reality.
The promise land is in sight. Equal rights in society;
No longer being called, a boy, a girl.
Live where heart desire.
Work where I have the education and the ability to do
so.
My promise land might not be the same as yours.
Hopes, dreams, reality, remain the same.

Let's not forget our black Moses that
saw the promise land of black and white holding
hands.
So today, stand tall with your Queen by your side,
with your future holding both your hands.
Speak with dignity, with honesty and with loyalty
to fight for the rights and welfare of all people.

Stand tall that man can look up to you.
Look in the eyes, but never over.
See the good in man;
the bad will remain in the shadow.
Use the love of Jesus to love the unloved.

You are our Joshua to both black and white.
As Dr. King was our black Moses.
It's not perchance that your roots are from two great
nations.
; take your place with the vision to bring into reality
'The Promise Land'
You are 'our **symbol of freedom**'

P.J.SCHLOSS

Today, Oh Wonderful Day

I see
Slaves dancing ,beating their drums,
blowing on their mouth pieces,
while forming a fence of love around you.
Freedom is here and they will not let it go.
It is in the air, in hearts that swell with pride,
in voices that shouted with laughter,
with feet that dance with joy.
Freedom is reality.

I see
Fredrick Douglas, Harriet Tubman, the famous,
the known and the unknown,
standing with hands lifted up to the heavens,
tears running down their cheeks.
Tears of joy flows for the past.
Tears that washed away regrets of the hearts.
Tears of joy that has found new love.
Tears of joy and relief for the present.

I see
This day for which our souls longed for.
This day old bones will crackle, joining
our people in dancing, and singing the song of
freedom, that
has been shut up in our beings.

I see
Dr. King and tens of thousands of men, women, boys
and girls
making a pathway for you to walk today.
Your walk to the white house,
is a symbol of our freedom.
We are so proud.

I see President Kennedy and Robert Kennedy waiting
with the door open wide for you to enter the White
House.
To fight for the rights of all people.

I see
Your parents holding hands,
forming an arch for you to walk under.
A symbol of two great nations,
coming together for such a time as this.
Their thoughts towards you are those of peace and
love,
some pride, but mostly grace for the task ahead.

I see
your grandparents holding hands. Smiling with the
expression
Of, "that our grandson, the symbol of freedom to all
men".
This is a moment that they wanted to share with each
other.

I see
People of every nation, every tribe, around the world
and here,
singing, dancing, praying
With great joy as you were sworn in today.

I see
Angels with bowed heads, thankful that God's will,
here on earth is fulfilled.
He heard the cries of the oppressed
and chose to answer on this day.
Yes, I know.
I was there and I saw.

"Oh, what a wonderful day"

PJ.>SCHLOSS

Inauguration Day

I Am Tired No More.

I see the slaves that labored to build the white house
standing with their scared backs.
Their broken spirits reflected in their downcast eyes,
their blood running to form
the pathway that you will walk on today.

You walk not only for us today,
but for them, whose sweat, tears and blood still
cries out for justice.

I see men of old standing with heads high
as their 'symbol of freedom' approaches.
Today they have become men.
They can look in the eyes of all.

I see them lifting you Sir,
'their symbol of freedom' over the tears,
blood ,sweat, lost dreams, hunger, un-forgiveness, and
anger
that line the steps to the White House.
Today you will be carried on the shoulders
of the men of old while they sing their song, *'I ain't tired
no more'*

It is now sung with a free heart with new meaning.
Free voices, free hearts,
They are not hungry
They are not homeless
They are not angry any more.
Justice is served today.

They have seen that their labored was not in vain.
They build the pathway for you today.
And you have taken it with great dignity.
"We tired no more, our whole being is now free."

P.J >SCHLOSS

'I ain't tired no more'

We Have Over Come

We have overcome
We have overcome this day.
We have seen the light.
We have seized the right.
Yes we have overcome this day.

No boy or girl
We have earned the right
To be heard around the world.
We have overcome this day.

Let's unite in voice
Let's unite in mind
Let's unite in strength
For we have overcome this day.

P.J> Schloss.

First And Only Lady

She stood by his side with love,
Honor, respect and trust.
Her love for him is transparent.
It is not hidden under the bushel.

She is proud to be the 'good thing' by his side.
And everyone to know it.
She is all woman to him and he knows it.
He lovingly sees her as his
Wife
Mother of his children
His friend
His lover
The one whose spirit is entwine with his.
His Queen
and
His First Lady.

PJ>Schloss.

Author's note

It was the summer of 2000 that I was commissioned by the many voices to write their cries. 'The Cries of Freedom, Past and Present' was birthed.

The many voices came in like a flood. It was like I was taken back in time to the day January 1, 1865. (My birthday is January 1) when freedom was proclaimed. I was compelled to listen to the men in the field, the young girl, the women in the house, the old man, the old woman , the young man; The families at the crossroad with their belongings on their heads, and the little boy running to his grandfather trying to understand the word, 'freedom'. He tried hard to contain the excitement of the day, least he wakes up to find it is all not true. They all wanted their stories told. They wanted people to know that freedom was welcomed, but not by all. Some were contented to remain slaves on the plantations, they were known as slaves, they lived as slaves, and they have become slaves. They never dreamed of any other type of life.

Mixed emotions were evident everywhere .With freedom came happiness, fear, helplessness, anger, hope, and loneliness. For some, revenge was still raw on the mind.

Some were fearful of further breakdown of the family unit or what was left of it. The fear of men leaving to seek better jobs in strange places became a reality, some never returned. Young men left, seeking the big cities with different motives, some joined gangs, and others found gainful hard work. There was no freedom from the lynching, no freedom from being called a 'nigger 'no freedom from being called a 'boy' or 'a girl'. They were free, but not free to become a man or a woman. Some knew that there was no freedom from looking at the pointed toe of the white man.

As is to be expected, for some there was no freedom from the revenge that was raw on the mind. Some lost their dreams, their hope, and their liberty because freedom did not find a way to their hearts. It was blocked with hate.

Yet freedom was embraced regardless of the hardship because with it came 'hope,' with hope, dreams can become a reality. Dreams give the will to live, not only for them but for us and for generations to come.

Today, we are living and will continue to live the dreams of 'freedom'.

NOTE:

Due to various unforeseen events I was unable to fulfill my goal to publish this book in a timely manner. However, it proves to be a good thing, because I had the great privilege to visit Africa – I went home. On arriving in Kenya, I experienced all the different emotions, especially when a total stranger approached me and said "welcome home"

I saw and experienced some of the rich culture of the land. I took in the vast beauty of the Rift Valley. Dancing with oldest tribe, the Maasai, that was a great thrill. I was educated in the culture of the different tribes. I breathed the air of my forefathers, I ate their food, I danced their dance and I fell in love with my kinfolk. I took the opportunity to include some pictures from my visit which I hope will create interest in wanting to know more about the 'Motherland' with a desire to visit.

IT'S OUR PAST THAT SHAPES OUR FUTURE; POSTIVE OR NEGATIVE.

The Whys Of The Poems

1. I came to the land of the unknown.
This poem is dedicated to the 4,000000 and more persons that were taken into slavery.

2. You never had me-----to --------Love is freedom.
These poems are the voices of the girl, the old man, the young boy, the old woman, the slave owner, the young man all sharing their emotions about freedom. These poems are all dedicated to them and their ancestor and descendants.

3. The struggle continues
A reminder of where we are coming from, to help young readers not to take freedom for granted.

4. Martin Luther King Jr. & Black Moses
Dedicated to a great man of peace, who knew his purpose and had a drive to fulfill it.

5. Blue Mountain Cries
This poem is dedicated to the land of my birth, Jamaica and to the peace loving people who are still living there.

6. How Can I Cry?
After reading,   'Cry The Beloved Country' by Alan Paton. I was so touched I wrote this poem. I dedicated this poem to the people of South Africa, where I would love to visit one day.

7. Without Roots and **We stand and Let.**
This is dedicated to the people of Sudan and to all the ladies I had the privilege of meeting in Kenya.

8. Cry My Beloved
This poem is also dedicated to the people of Jamaica.

9. Bondage

This is dedicated to all the people who have had to flee their home land in Africa.

10. **The Promise Land.**
This is dedicated to Mr. Barack Obama , I wrote this poem when he was elected as the Presidential nominee; **My symbol of freedom.**

11. **'Today, Oh wonderful day'.**
This dedicated to everyone who witness this day of history.

12. **I Am Tired No More.**
This is dedicated to all the men of old who built the White House.

!3. **We have overcome**
To all who felt that we have cross over on this day January 20th 2009.

14. **First and Only Lady.**
Dedicated to Mrs. Michelle Obama, 'Our First Lady'.

About the Author

PAULINE J. SCHLOSS has written and published other books such as, 'He Cares for me, The Voice of the Heart, and The Heart Speaks.' Ms.Schloss also wrote 'Tithing or Tipping', a book on the principles of tithing and giving.

Ms.Schloss lives in South Florida. She is the mother of six children and grandmother of three beautiful girls and two grandsons. Her passions are traveling, fulfilling the great commission, writing and cooking.

www.ingramcontent.com/pod-product-compliance
Lightning Source LLC
Chambersburg PA
CBHW031252280526
45784CB00004B/1827